My Son His Son

A Mother's Journey Through the Chaos of Rebellion

Susan Jill Ream

www.timelesspublications.co.uk

Timeless Publlications Ltd., Castlerock, Northern Ireland
All rights reserved. This book or any portion thereof may
not be reproduced or used in any manner whatsoever without the express written permission of the publisher except
for the use of brief quotations in a book review.

CONTENTS

Preface

Are you trying to cope with a rebellious teen? Does your child display characteristics of oppositional defiant disorder? Do you feel hopeless, distraught, confused, and alone? I felt all of these emotions and more in my plight as a mom raising a rebel son.

I wrote My Son His Son from my heart. It is my story of desperately seeking God in the midst of utter chaos. I share my story, including not only the struggles but key truths I learned along the way to living through desperate days. But for the grace of God I would have given up in despair. God proved to be my everything, and as the Hound of Heaven, he continually chased down my son.

My son, Daniel, blessed my life with immeasurable joy, but he also brought the most profound pain I have ever experienced. For those who are clinging to sanity while your teen is spiraling out of control and to those who come behind me, I hold out a torch, urging you to run to Jesus because he holds the answers to all your questions.

Be brave, dearest Mom and weary Dad, as you wait on God, who will never leave you or let go of your child.

Trust in the Lord with all your heart,
and do not lean on your own
understanding.
Proverbs 3:5 (ESV)

Introduction

As long as I can remember, my deepest desire in life was to be the best mother possible. When I came to know the Lord at age fifteen, I felt sure God would enable me to fulfill that yearning. I also believed that when I had children, he would cocoon them and keep them safe. I had dreams of nurturing and raising each of my little ones to claim Christ unashamedly and to live a surrendered life. I believed that the next generation of Reams would carry on our legacy of living out Christianity through ministry.

Looking back, I'd say I had God tucked neatly into a little box with a beautiful bow tied around it. I had much to learn about Father God, my Creator and Sustainer, and of his Son, the Savior, whose boundless mercy and grace never failed me. Through a multitude of messes, God led me to release my white-knuckled grip on my teenage son so that God could do what only he can do.

I grew up in a dysfunctional home. Insecurity, hostility, neglect, and lack of love were my reality as a child. I was disillusioned with life until God miraculously reached down and saved me as a teenager. My life after salvation was a series of miracles. I had come to depend on and believe in God's generosity, goodness, and grace. I had a before and after picture of my new life in Christ that looked more like a fairy tale than a pilgrim's journey. I had not yet experienced the testing of my faith or witnessed the hand of God in the midst of darkness.

My belief was that God would protect my children from all harm and certainly bless our family with the happy home I had dreamed of as a child. Through the long and arduous process of suffering and loss of a dream, God revealed himself as Provider, Redeemer, Comforter, Stronghold, and Unchangeable Father.

My Son His Son

A new love was birthed the day my son was born, the unfathomable love known only to a mother. I awoke each morning enveloped in anticipation and wonder.

Eagerness filled me as I reached to hold my little miracle. I studied him with a desire to uncover all of the mysteries hidden within. When my son looked at me, with his whole face crinkled up in a smile, my heart melted. As I took my first baby steps into the world of parenting, the idea of raising a rebellious teenager never entered my mind.

As my little man grew, he walked away from me and into the world where danger and evil lurked. I watched him run recklessly toward independence in all the wrong ways. I went through years of countless tears, intense pain, and pleading prayers for my boy.

When our firstborn entered puberty and sent our world

into a tailspin, I was stunned to be thrown into the chaotic world of stressed-out parents raising rebellious teens. I had given birth to a precious boy who, upon adolescence, turned into an argumentative, defiant, oppositional teenager.

Daniel's temper became explosive. How could we provide a safe place for our two girls when our son disrupted the whole family? We never knew when the next eruption would occur. With each new outburst, I found myself staring at my son in disbelief. I wondered what we did wrong and how this craziness could happen to us.

Parenting teenagers, even in the best of situations, is hard. Parenting a teen caught in the storm of rebellion is a nightmare. To keep our heads and hearts above the tempest, we needed the kind of wisdom that only God's grace could provide. We required a close connection to God to get through these turbulent years.

My son's rebellion began when he was twelve years old and extended way beyond the teen years and well into his thirties. I don't think there is a weary parent living today who can say teenage rebellion is something they were prepared to face or qualified to handle. I may have been the least prepared mom in the world when defiance took up residence in my son's heart.

One day as I prayed for Daniel, I heard a clear message from my Father God: This boy you call your son is my son first. Letting those words sink deep into my soul, I experienced peace for the first time in years. Slowly God released me from the fear and deep pain that had been consuming my life.

I finally got it! Father God loved my son much more than I was capable of loving.

God urged me to let go and let him take over. Turning from my own reasoning and resources to complete dependence on and a deep trust in God opened my spiritual eyes. It was then I witnessed God's relentless pursuit of my son's heart. A chase ensued as God's works were revealed in the most miraculous ways. My boy could not outrun God's amazing love.

My son is an adult now, and I am so proud of the man he has become. He'd run into brick walls repeatedly, but eventually (many years' worth of eventualities) he allowed his trials to weave strength into the fabric of his being. Join me as I reveal glimpses of my life as a mother of a prodigal. Feel the emotions that threatened to overtake me and render me useless. Be astounded by the hand of God showing up over and over again in the midst of the mess. Witness the God of miracles touch my son and change a double-minded young man into a fervent follower of Jesus.

Don't allow yourself to get swallowed up in hopelessness. Remember Jesus's words: "I will never leave you or forsake you" (Heb. 13:5).

I share my story in hopes of encouraging moms, dads, and all those who pray for and love a teenager bent on destruction.

As you walk your journey through rebellion, let me encourage you to stay faithful to the One who loves your child most. God will use your story when you get to the other side and begin to see God's hand all over the years of your confusion and pain. "Blessed be the God and Father of our Lord Jesus Christ, the Father of mercies and God of all comfort who comforts us in all of our affliction, so that we may be able to comfort those who are in any affliction, with the comfort with which we ourselves are comforted by God" (2 Cor. 1:3–4).

I praise God for teaching me that he is God and I am not. I pray my personal story touches your life and gives you courage and peace should you face the day your child walks away from your heart.

A Few More Words Just for You

1. Remember, your child is on loan. He or she is first and foremost God's child, and he is faithful. Trust him!

2. Be prepared to do battle against the Enemy, who will fight for your child's heart.

3. Put on the armor of God: "Put on the whole armor of God, that you may be able to stand against the schemes of the devil. For we do not wrestle against flesh and blood, but against the rulers, against the authorities, against the cosmic powers over this present darkness, against the spiritual forces of evil in the heavenly places" (Eph. 6:11–12).

4. Stay close to the Father. He is faithful and will teach you through the storm.

Reflections B.C. (Before Children)

1

When I was in college, I viewed from afar a very handsome young man named Gary, the exemplification of everything I had ever dreamed of in a husband. He was kind, strong, smart, and he loved the Lord. He was a leader on campus and the music director at the local church I attended. I was in his choir.

I never thought Gary noticed me, but one day he surprised me by sitting next to me during a church service. I was a wreck being in such close proximity to this young man I had elevated near the angels.

When he glanced at me, I felt the heat rise in my cheeks. He touched the pearl ring on my left hand and asked, "What does that ring mean to you?"

My mouth went dry as I looked down at my promise ring from my boyfriend back home.

Gary didn't know that in the quietness of each night, I had been wrestling with God about this ring. He was convicting me to break my bond with this boy because he was not a spiritual leader.

"I don't know right now," I answered meekly. Only

Mary, my trusted friend and roommate, knew of the battles that had been taking place within me. She'd heard my weeping and would get out of bed, hug me, and listen to my struggle. I knew what God wanted me to do, but I didn't want to give up my boyfriend, my best friend. I fought with God alone, but Gary's question left me feeling exposed.

After church that night, Gary walked me back to the dorm. I allowed the butterflies within to fill me with joy. I was thankful to spend time with my ideal.

When Gary returned to his dorm, he grabbed his Resident Advisor, Terry. "I met this girl tonight, and I'm going to marry her! But there's one problem. She's pre-engaged." He continued in earnest. "We need to pray she breaks up with this guy." Gary told Terry his plans. "This is the one, Terry. After this year, I'm going to give her a promise ring, and during our junior year, I will give her a diamond. I want to marry her after our junior year."

Believe it or not, that's just what happened. Terry told me later that he never doubted Gary but prayed in agreement with him.

A few weeks after Gary's question, I made the dreaded call to my guy back home. He was heartbroken, as was I.

During the months that followed, he called repeatedly, pleading for answers as to why I had taken such drastic action. If I told him that God had revealed my need for a spiritual leader, he surely would have tried, in his own strength, to be that for me. But I had to know if his faith was real and if God would use our breakup to grab his attention. Throughout the devastation of losing my best friend, God brought peace. I obeyed him and that's all that mattered.

Meanwhile, Gary continued to pursue me. I was still in awe that my "idol" was interested in me. As I worked through the aftermath of my breakup with my high school sweetheart, he listened attentively, lifting my spirits when I felt sad. He prayed for me and showed great compassion.

This was the beginning of our ever-after. Gary modeled a love for Christ, which drew me in quickly, and his unconditional love for me touched me in a way I had never known.

As our relationship deepened, we talked about our future and our thoughts on marriage and parenting. We observed the pain and insecurity firmly planted in children who were neglected. We were also aware of the opposite parenting style. Overprotective parenting resulted in kids who were not ready to face the world.

Naturally, as wise as we were, we knew we would raise the perfect children. Without knowing it, we set ourselves up for disillusionment and deep disappointment. We were naïve and shamefully proud in our understanding of parenting.

A Few More Words Just for You

1. When you commit your life to Christ, expect him to direct your path. Blessings follow obedience.

2. Parenting looks simple before you have kids. Don't assume you hold all the answers.

In all your ways acknowledge him, and he will make straight your paths. Proverbs 3:6 (ESV)

Our First Church Ministry

2

After three years of dating the love of my life, I walked down the aisle and married him. I went to work to pay the bills as Gary finished his schooling. After he graduated with a major in Religious Education and a minor in Music, Gary accepted the position as pastor of Christian Education as well as Youth and Music at a church in Amherst, Ohio.

This first ministry kept us both busy. We thrived in our calling: he as a pastor and me as counselor, teacher, and friend to the youth. Once a week teens filled our house. Throughout the week, the kids randomly stopped by to hang out and talk. Laughter and long talks ensued into the night with these teens. We created strong bonds with our teens—some relationships exist to this day.

Life was filled with happy days of laughter, adventures, and growth. About fourteen months after our wedding, as we were actively serving in Amherst, Ohio, we learned I was pregnant with our first child. Secretly, I hoped for a boy to lead his siblings. We were elated when Daniel, our chubby-cheeked, curly-haired little boy, arrived. I spent hours studying my little man. Wonder filled me. This child was mine!

Twenty-two months after his birth and to my delight, our first daughter, Renee, was born. Her quiet nature and feminine characteristics were in stark contrast to her brother, who whizzed through the house like a reckless tornado, dismantlng everything he touched.

Our rambunctious Daniel was the center of attention at church and youth group. The teens competed to hold him. As a toddler, Daniel was a charmer. He loved being with the teens. All smiles, dimpled cheeks, and high fives made him the preferred toddler in the church.

Though charming, he was also strong willed, which showed up early in his life. To teach him the concept of obedience, I left a few do-not-touch pieces within his reach. When he began to toddle toward one of these items, I would say firmly, "No, Daniel!" He would look at me, at first in confusion, then continue on to gain the thing he had set his mind on. In response I paddled his cushioned behind and pulled him back. His determination was relentless. I was consistant, but the battle continued.

As time went on, his determination escalated. In response to my warning, "Daniel, do not touch!" not only did he head for the do-not-touch prize, but he broke out in a big smile as he ran to secure victory over my command. Each time he disobeyed, he endured a consequence. He cried and hugged me, shook it off, then ran right back to the object—every time!

We used a variety of consequences, but the goal, in

Daniel's mind, was always the same: "I'm going to get the prize no matter what you say!" Eventually, I used distraction rather than confrontation. It prevented a showdown and kept the peace for many years.

Daniel's obstinate behavior was opposite of my girls' when they were this same age. When I said, "No," they would back away and redirect on their own.

Because Daniel was my firstborn, I was naïve about children and behaviors. I did not perceive that his actions were warnings of something deeper at work. I thought he was starting the so-called terrible twos earlier than normal. But his determination and resolute commitment to defy my commands foreshadowed things to come.

A Few More Words Just for You

1. If your child is strong willed, equip yourself with Christian resources on parenting. Strong-willed children will push limits. Children need boundaries, which provide a sense of security. Keep your boundaries firm.

2. A resource for raising strong willed children is, *Temper Your Child's Tantrum,* by Dr. James Dobson. Dr. Dobson is a well-known and trusted Psychologist in the Christian arena. If you need strategies for maintaining a calm and peaceful home, this book is for you.

Train up a child in the way he should go; even when he is old he will not depart from it.
Proverbs 22:6 (ESV)

Our Second Church Ministry

3

A fter four years of ministry in Ohio, Gary went back to seminary in Grand Rapids, Michigan. Daniel was three, and Renee, one and a half.

At the end of Gary's second year of seminary, he planned to enroll for year three when a pastor on the East side of Michigan contacted him. One of Gary's professor's recommended him to the senior pastor of this church. After we candidated, the church voted to bring Gary on staff as their Christian Education, Youth, and Music Pastor.

Though I was eight months pregnant with our third child, we packed up our belongings, spread our wings, and took off for a new adventure. A month later, I gave birth to our bundle of joy, Christine, a bubbly, happy baby. She brought so much joy into our family. Daniel and Renee often vied for her attention. Christy completed our family.

Daniel was growing in age and maturity. As he grew, obstinacy took a backseat as a sweet little boy emerged. Though my son continued to be strong willed, his heart was kind. He had a firm conviction of honesty. When he spoke, his words always proved to be true. Daniel loved Jesus and told people what he did for him and for them. One day, at about the age of five, he said, "Mama, I went to Mr. Jack's house today."

Curious, I asked, "You did, honey? Why did you go to his house?"

"I knocked on his door, and when he came out, I asked if he knew Jesus, and asked if he knew Jesus died so he could go to heaven."

"Wow, buddy, that's cool! What did he say?"

"Well, he just smiled at me and said he had to go because something was on the stove."

This bold yet simple act revealed his heart of compassion and faith.

As Daniel grew older, he memorized so many scriptures that he won the Timothy Award in our church's Awana program. I knew that even at this young age, God had his hand on my son's life.

We enrolled Daniel in a local Christian school kindergarten. Our desire was to provide him with the best education and atmosphere possible. In the early years of school, he struggled to stay in his seat. Daniel's first grade teacher told us he wiggled all the time. She said he was either flipped under his desk, sitting on top of it, or studying the mechanics underneath. He could not seem to keep his bottom where it belonged.

About halfway through first grade he began to stutter. It was painful and disconcerting to watch him struggle to get his words out. What was happening to my boy? The teacher, who was frustrated with Daniel, advised us to have him evaluated. The school recommended a Christian social worker.

The social worker was a warm, kind, and gentle man. Among the many strategies he applied was storytelling. As he told Daniel stories, he instructed him to draw pictures. Daniel loved spending time with him. In the end, the evaluator said that Daniel was very unique, that he was no "cookie cutter kid." He told us that Daniel learned in a different way from most children. He explained that the Christian school we had him in was too restrictive for his personality. "The kids in this school are like little wooden soldiers who march to a very rigid drum. Your son marches to a different drumbeat."

He recommended taking him out of school every other day and homeschooling him on his days off. The goal was to reduce Daniel's pressure. It worked, for he thrived at home. His stuttering stopped, and he returned to being a happy little boy.

Looking back, I am thankful the Christian school directed me to a wonderful counselor who guided us down the right path for our son. Taking him out of the school because the atmosphere was too restrictive for him was the right choice. Years later, and in the midst of turmoil, I remembered the evaluator's words and realized how profound they were. My son was no cookie-cutter kid.

A Few More Words Just For You

1. If your child is struggling at school, seek professional guidance.

2. Be aware that children learn differently.

3. Know your child. Study his or her personality and observe how he or she learns.

4. I recommend the book The Way They Learn by Cynthia Ulrich Tobias.

5. Teach your child to memorize God's Word, for it will follow him or her for life. If you have a church nearby with an Awana program, I encourage you to enroll your child in it.

6. Understand that not all schools are equal. They vary widely in curriculum and teaching methods. We have two excellent Christian schools in our area. One is rigid and controlled. Their training and focus, apart from general education, is to equip children to live for Christ. The other school's atmosphere is of love and acceptance. They embrace differences in kids. They, too, are focused on equipping their students to serve Christ, understanding that each child is unique. Some children thrive with a rigid structure while others shrivel in this

kind of learning environment, feeling constricted and possibly like failures.

7. Remember that you are your child's advocate.

You are your Child's Best Advocate

Our Third Church Ministry

4

When Daniel was nine years old, my husband received a request to consider pastoring a church in Illinois. After visiting the church and interviewing with the committee, Gary received a unanimous call to be their pastor.

Prior to this, my father was diagnosed with cancer and did not have long to live. We lived forty-five minutes from him. I stayed involved in his treatment options and provided feedback in the decisions he had to make. I took him to most of his appointments and discussed his care with medical professionals.

If we accepted the call, we would have to move six hours away from Dad. I would no longer be able to assist him. Gary asked me what I thought about moving to Illinois.

"Honey, my dad is sick. I don't know what to do. You make the decision and I will follow your lead."

He lifted my chin and peered into my eyes. "Not this time, sweetheart. I will not make this decision alone. You must also feel called."

Gary asked the church for time to pray and seek God's

will.

I talked with my dad and explained the situation. "Dad, last weekend Gary and I went to Illinois to candidate at a church. The church voted to extend an invitation to Gary. The vote was unanimous. They want Gary as their pastor." I paused a moment as tears welled in my eyes. "But, Dad, I don't want to leave you."

My dad smiled and patted my hand. "Susie, you go with your husband. I want you to follow the Lord. It seems to me God has opened this door for your family."

I felt his blessing and a release. I prayed God would equip my mom and siblings to care for him as carefully and intentionally as I had.

Believing this was God's leading, we packed up our belongings and relocated from Michigan to Illinois.

Gary's position was Senior Pastor, but he also served in this small country church as a worship leader, choir director, youth pastor, janitor, electrician, builder—you name it, he did it. At first, Daniel seemed to adjust well to our new life.

Once again, our house was abuzz with teens. We invited them into our home and to be part of our family. What we did not see at the time was the effect these teens had on our preadolescent boy. Daniel was watching carefully and being influenced by some of the rebellious teens in the group.

Another of my misconceptions uncovered! I thought if we immersed ourselves in ministry, our children would be protected. But ministry does not guarantee some sort of magical blanket will cover your family. In fact, the Enemy targets those who are making an impact for the kingdom. I share this as a warning. Though we felt compelled to reach out to the youth, we did not protect our son in doing so. We did not even realize the impact of the exposure to rebels would have on him.

We could have ministered to the kids in town while protecting our children. We could have met at the church and employed a trusted babysitter. We didn't see the danger. It was in this small-town church that rebellion and chaos entered our lives.

A Few More Words Just for You

1. Tune in to your children; they are your first responsibility. Understand that they are like sponges and have not yet learned to discern between fun and rebellion.

2. Be aware that protection applies not only to the physical realm. Protect your children from situations and people who might harm them or negatively influence their minds.

But they did not obey or incline their ear, but walked in their own counsels and the stubbornness of their evil hearts, and went backward and not forward.
Jeremiah 7:24 (ESV)

Growing in Rebellion

5

The first signs of trouble came when Daniel, then twelve, began to display passive-aggressive behavior. When asked to do something, he would stubbornly, yet silently, refuse to do it. If I said, "Daniel, clean your room and bring me your laundry," he stared at me without answering. I didn't understand his behavior. I remember thinking, People say kids go though stages. I hope this one passes soon.

His quiet rebellion was met with consequences. "Daniel, when I speak to you, you need to answer me, okay?" No response. So I sent him to his room with an admonition: "Son, when you are ready to talk to me and cooperate, you may come out." Sometimes we took away his baseball card collection, grounded him from his friends, or revoked television privileges. We took away privilege after privilege, but nothing seemed to matter to him.

He stayed in his room and sat alone. He ignored everyone. I thought eventually he would grow tired of his isolation, but he did not. We were distressed and clueless, not knowing how to get through to this boy who refused to cooperate.

I tried reasoning. "Daniel, do you really think refusing to do what you are told is worth it? Don't you want to play with your friends, watch TV, and join in with the family? What are you thinking, son?" He stared into my eyes but spoke not a word. I tried again. "Son, I am not asking you to lift a mountain here. If you would just do as you are asked, your life will be so much better." Again no answer. It seemed he shut down. Whenever I tried to engage him in a conversation, I got the same response.

During a family vacation with friends, his silent rebellion manifested and ruined it for all of us. On the first day, Daniel refused to cooperate. "Hey, Daniel, will you take the cold stuff out of the trunk and put it in the fridge?" He stood still staring at me, refusing to speak. I was embarrased and alarmed that he acted up in front of our dear family friends. Gary and I were looking forward to a break from the rat race, but instead we were faced with the complexity of not knowing how to handle his behavior. Our friends were also baffled.

As always, we gave him a consequence. "Son, you need to do as you are told. Go to your tent until you can apologize for ignoring me." He went to his tent willingly, but he never apologized and, consequently, never came out.

We went to the lake without him; we sat by the fire while he peeked out at us. Sometimes I heard him chuckle from his tent as he listened to our family stories. He refused to admit he was wrong or to say, "I am sorry."

Gary and I felt the heaviness of not knowing how to

help our son. We grieved the loss of a fun family vacation. We felt horrible for our friends, who had anticipated a sweet time of fellowship with us but instead got pulled into our brokeness.

After we returned from vacation, we found a Christian counselor to help us wade through the tough stuff. But before we got too far into our sessions, I found a notebook in Daniel's room. Grabbing it, I searched for clues about what was going on inside my boy's head. What I found blew me away. The pages were filled with lyrics, dark and oppressive words glorifying evil, death, and suicide. We realized we needed more help, a different level of help, than what the counselor could provide.

Although we lived in Illinois, my friend Cathy and I drove to Texas to have Daniel evaluated by a counselor at a well-known Christian clinic. We were surprised to learn that counseling for Daniel would require an extended amount of time. Cathy drove back by herself, and Gary came down to be with me the following week. Daniel's counseling excluded us. Our son was thirteen and subject to client-counselor confidentiality.

One day when Gary and I picked up Daniel after an appointment, he confronted us. "You guys can't tell me what to do anymore! I'm sick of being made to follow your stupid rules!" He expressed his disdain with fierce profanity.

We could hardly believe the obscenities that spewed from Daniel's mouth. Gary and I felt numb and in shock. Our silent son had turned to verbally abusing us. He went on to justify himself. "My counselor told me to get my words out. He told me to swear and to use any words I needed to get my anger out. He said to tell you off if it helped me."

The rest of that ride was like our worst nightmare. While the counselor had led Daniel out of his silent rebellion, he taught him to communicate with blatant, in-your-face rebellion. Our son used his words to slam and shatter us. He cussed at us and justified it all by naming the counselor as his support. We were not prepared for this switch in his personality. We teetered between wanting to smack him to stopping the car and demanding he get out and walk. How could our son change so drastically?

I called the clinic with an urgent request to speak with the doctor in charge. Dr. Warren met Gary and me after reading Daniel's evaluation. We told him what had occurred on our ride home, including what Daniel had said transpired between his counselor and him.

Alarm spread across Dr. Warren's face. "This is not the way we counsel our teens!" Clearly, he believed our account. "This will be dealt with, I promise you!"

We believe Daniel's counselor was fired, because we no longer heard him as a speaker on the clinic's radio show, but the harm was already done. Daniel felt empowered.

We were shocked by Dr. Warren's advice. "I am recommending you take Daniel to a safe place while he works through his mood swings and rebellion. He is in a very destructive condition."

How did my silent son suddenly become destructive?

Dr. Warren interrupted my thoughts. "I just met with a young man, Mark Gregston, who is the founder of a Christian home for troubled youth. It's called Heartlight, located in Longview, Texas." Dr. Warren paused before continuing. "I believe in Mark's ministry and highly recommend you take Daniel to Heartlight."

Gary and I struggled to process what he was suggesting. We thought if we took our son to these experts, they would help us fix him. We were so naïve!

A Few More Word Just for You

1. Bad counsel can come from well-known and reputable counseling services.

2. Insist on keeping a close connection with any counselor who talks to your child. If you see anything abnormal, pull your child, then contact and meet with the head of the organization.

Do not be deceived

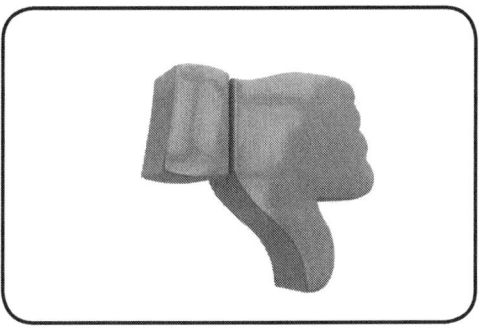

bad company **ruins** good morals
1 Corinthians 15:33 (ESV)

Heartlight

6

As a mom, I was devastated with this current situation, but I believed we must follow the recommendation of this respected Christian psychologist.

Daniel had just turned thirteen and was going to live far away from home. Driving him to Longview, Texas, knowing we would be leaving him there, ripped at my heart. My soul cried out, "God, this isn't the way it's supposed to be!" Yet Dr. Warren had cautioned us, "If you take Daniel home, you will lose him." We did not fully understand this ominous warning or the wisdom his words held. We simply chose to trust Dr. Warren's expertise.

Arriving at the Heartlight ranch, I took in the vast beauty and peace surrounding me. We drove down a long driveway through rolling hills. Before we arrived at the lodge, we spotted a large tennis court, a sparkling blue swimming pool, and a barn filled with well-groomed horses. Everything was cradled within beautiful tall pines.

Entering the main living area, I felt impressed. It was spacious and tastefully decorated! The log home was filled with grand, comfy furniture.

At any other time I would have been in awe of this gorgeous retreat. I saw it all, yet there was a disconnect. I was numb. I could not feel. It was surreal.

Mark and Jan Gregston welcomed us warmly. Jan smiled as Mark said, "Come on in, guys. It's great to have you here." Mark looked past us and grabbed Daniel's hand. "Hey, buddy, my name is Mark. It's good to meet you." Daniel gave a slight smile and shook his hand. "How about we take a tour of Heartlight?"

We knew almost immediately that Mark and Jan were good people. As Mark showed us around, he told us their history of working with teens. When he shared past stories and experiences, wisdom and passion poured out of this young man. He loved the Lord and had a calling to help troubled teens. We were convinced the Gregston's held a fierce commitment to kids in trouble—the more we listened the deeper our belief. Firm boundaries were in place at Heartlight. Jan and Mark invested their hearts in the kids entrusted to their care. Though Mark's words were reassuring, the knot in my stomach persisted. Tears were so close to the surface. I worked hard to keep them in check. Then I felt my emotions shutting down.

After walking with Daniel to his room, we prepared to leave. Everything in me wanted to grab my son and run! But I knew if we took him home with the new new "skills" he had learned from his counselor, chaos would erupt and destroy our home.

Leaving Daniel at Heartlight was devastating. Who

does this? I knew we had no alternative, but I could not process turning over my just-turned thirteen-year-old son to another's care.

On our long, mostly silent, ride home, we prayed and asked God to help our son and bless the Gregstons. We were grief striken.

After arriving home we called Mark. We learned that Daniel was making adjustments. Beginning with a soft chuckle, Mark explained, "I have to tell you a story about your son. I walked in on Daniel as he was swinging a baseball bat at his mattress. So I said, 'Hey, there, buddy, what are you doing?'

"'I'm getting my anger out!' Daniel explained."

The counselor who had taught Daniel to use his words also encouraged him to hit something when he was angry.

"So I said, Son, we don't deal with anger this way at Heartlight. What are you going to do someday when you get angry at your wife? Are you going to hit her?'"

That ended the bat-bashing sessions.

Another incident sent Daniel running from the lodge in a rage. Something had ticked him off. Mark sent some staff and a couple of the bigger boys to tackle him and hold him down until he stopped his fit. In that moment, Daniel learned that flying off the handle didn't work at Heartlight. Gary and I were impressed by Mark's wisdom in dealing with Daniel.

Throughout the school year at Heartlight, Daniel gradually learned to control his temper and enter into community. He took part in chores, even had his own horse to care for. He learned how to respect his authorities and get along with his comrades. The kids developed a tight bond. They enjoyed many fun and educational experiences, but they also carried some heavy-duty, grown-up responsibilities.

Daniel understood why he was there, yet he wanted to be back with his family. We longed to have him home. He worked hard to earn the privilege to return home.

One day Mark called us to share something special about Daniel. He said that from time to time, as the group was involved in a Bible study, Daniel piped up with a correction or a supportive passage from the Bible. Daniel even led the kids to turn to the Scripture reference. Mark said, "I think Dan knows the Bible better than any of us."

Remember those years of Awana training? Scripture does not return void. But it also goes to show you that a person can know the Scriptures in his head, but until it reaches his heart, it does not change the person.

God says that the Bible is alive and sharper than any two-edged sword (Heb. 4:12), and although Daniel's ear was not inclined to the Word, it never left him.

Our son spent almost one year at Heartlight. It was an invaluable, life-changing experience for him. To this day, I see strengths God placed in Daniel because of the training and time invested in him. Mark Gregston left a stamp of his good ol' boy manliness on his life. Daniel deeply admires and respects him to this day.

A Few More Words Just for You

1. If a trusted Christian counselor gives you hard advice, though everything in you screams no, pray. If God directs you to trust the professional, follow his or her direction.

2. Know that if the time comes to leave your child in another's care, God will not leave your child.

...but they who wait for the Lord
shall renew their strength;
they shall mount up with
wings like eagles;
they shall run and not be weary;
they shall walk and not faint.
Isaiah 40:1 (ESV)

The Waiting Game

7

During Daniel's time at Heartlight, my heart ached every day for the loss and incredible disillusionment of my life as a parent. Some days I sat by a window—never moving and never saying a word. My emotions were frozen, therefore I felt frozen. It was as if my world had stopped. I could not move or participate in life. When this behavior persisted beyond a reasonable period, my husband became alarmed. He contacted my Christian physician.

The doctor listened to Gary and shared his concern. Then he recommended a presciption for an antidepressant. My husband said, "Susie will never take medication for depression. She doesn't believe in taking antidepressants."

In response, my doctor told my husband to put me on the phone. He didn't mince words. "Susan, I want you to go on an antidepressant." I started to argue, but he interrupted me. "If you do not do what I recommend, you will end up in a place where you will not be able to take care of your other children."

That got through to me.

"Okay. I'll do it."

Before this incident, my position on antidepressants was that if you had faith in God, you would not need antidepressants.

My discerning physician knew I needed the medication for this very dark period of my life. The medication unlocked my frozen emotions. I could then think, function, and care for my girls

God was teaching me, even in the midst of my desperate state of mind. I was in a position where I had to accept what I needed, including an antidepressant. As a result, I have great compassion for others and do not judge people who find themselves in a very dark place and need the help of a medication.

As my mind cleared, I dug into the Word of God and clung to it as to life itself. It had never failed to direct me. Yet I had not been tested in some areas of life application.

Did I believe God's promises? For instance, "And we know God works all things together for our good" (Rom. 8:28, author's paraphrase). If I had birthed perfect kids, if my faith had not been tested, if God had not walked me through the darkness, would I have grasped the depth of faith it takes to actually know that God is working all things together for my good? I was learning that God works through the good, the bad, and the ugly circumstances of life.

Now that my brain was working, I had to find a job to help support Daniel at Heartlight. Even though Gary and I desired that I be a stay-at-home mother (the hand that rocks the cradle rules the world), my husband's income was not sufficient for our needs. I went to work full time at a weight-loss clinic. My employer sent me for training as a nutritioinal specialist and a behavior breakthrough counselor. I truly loved my job and the people. When I worked, I was distracted from the load of pain I carried. But on my journey home each day, I picked it back up. The antidepressants enabled me to move and to function, for which I am most grateful, but they could not heal the brokenness inside.

All of my income went to support Daniel's stay at Heartlight. In addition to what I earned, my husband's parents and a very dear couple, our faithful friends, sacrificed to make my son's stay at Heartlight possible. Though it was costly financially, it was an investment worth every penny.

I felt desperately broken every single day as I waited for my son's return home. I continually struggled to grasp what had happened. I analyzed every situation of our lives and all of our parenting efforts, trying to identify our parenting flaws.

I never doubted God, but I questioned my understanding of who he is. I struggled with believing he would pull my son through. I carried all the weight on my shoulders, and that weight almost destroyed me emotionally and physically.

A Few More Words Just for You

1. Expect Trials. If you are a child of God, expect trials. "Beloved, do not be surprised at the fiery trial when it comes upon you to test you, as though something strange were happening to you" (1 Peter 4:12).

2. Trials prove the genuineness of your faith. "In all this you greatly rejoice, though now for a little while you may have had to suffer grief in all kinds of trials. These have come so that the proven genuineness of your faith—of greater worth than gold, which perishes even though refinded by fire—may result in praise, glory and honor when Jesus Christ is revealed" (1:6–7).

3. Trials produce endurance. "For you know that the testing of your faith produces steadfastness" (James 1:3).

Returning Home

8

After almost a year of waiting, the day finally arrived for Daniel to come home. It was a time of joyous celebration. Our summer was packed full of fun. Daniel enthusiastically entered our family outings. We enjoyed a vacation, family trips, and church events. Daniel was determined and resolute in his commitment to walk a different walk. We were so hopeful. He was changed. All was well . . . or so we thought.

Enter fall, which you can define as autumn or as to stumble or stray. Daniel entered his first year of high school with a conviction to stay strong and not bend to bad influences. However, it wasn't long before I knew he was spiraling downhill like a plane nose-diving to its demise. His decline was so sharp and fast that it threw our family into a state of distress and confusion.

Daniel began staying out late. Sometimes we didn't know where he was. One time Gary reached out to a faithful deacon for help in finding Daniel. Together they scoured the city to find him and drag him back home.

Daniel was hanging out with some rebellious kids and quickly picking up their way of life. His confrontational behavior and filthy language, encouraged by his Texas counselor, returned. I was terrified as I witnessed him going down the slippery slope he eagerly embraced. The rebel teens in town actively pursued Daniel. When they came to our house asking to see him, I was shocked and answered firmly, "No, I am sorry. Daniel may not come out."

These teens were brazen and bold. They even came to our church on a Sunday or Wednesday night, trying to make contact with my son. Gary and I were stunned as we watched a group of teens, dressed like gang members, file into the church and take seats in the back of the sanctuary. On these occasions, my pastor-husband walked to the church porch and poured his heart out to God. He begged God to help him. In the flesh he wanted to demand these aggressive pursuers out of the church and away from our son; instead, he walked back in and presented a salvation message. He prayed God would touch just one of their hearts.

As I witnessed the teens'pursuit of my son and his growing rebellion, panic swelled within me. I was frightened.

Our church family handled all this craziness with great patience and love; it humbled us. These dear folks loved our son, and they loved and supported us. They were available to help whenever we asked. I remember one Sunday morning a faithful deacon, Tom, came to get Daniel out of bed. He went into his bedroom and said, "Daniel, get up, son. It's time for church." Surprisingly, Daniel got up and went to church.

I have heard heartbreaking stories from parents of rebellious kids. As the family faces the hardest days of their lives, some churches gossip, blame, and criticize the parents. I thank God for placing us in a body of Christ followers who believed in us as parents. They believed in God as the blessed controller of all things, and they chose to love our son in spite of his behavior. I can confidently say it was this consistent love from the people of our congregation that kept Daniel from never turning against the church.

As the school year progressed, Daniel's destructive behavior continued to circle downward. One day, when I was particularly distressed, I asked Gary if we could pray for our son every hour on the hour while he was at school. We set our alarms and did just that. We stormed heaven's gates and pleaded for our son and for protection from evil. We prayed specifically for things like his smoking in school and his temper. After school that day, I casually asked Daniel, "How was your day, son?"

"It was strange."

"How do you mean?"

"Well, between classes this morning, I stopped by the bathroom for a smoke, but as soon as I took that first drag, I got sick and threw up. I left but tried again later. Every time I tried to smoke, I vomited. It was really weird." He wore a look of puzzlement. "Something else happened, and I don't get it!"

"What happened?" I asked.

"This kid in my science class deliberately pushed my buttons. Any other time, it would have set me off. I probably would have punched him in the face, but I couldn't even feel anger." He shook his head and started to walk away.

I stopped him. I didn't want him to miss this revelation of the power of prayer. I told him how his dad and I had joined together and prayed over him that whole day. His face revealed astonishment as he turned to walk away. He remembers this incident as a powerful lesson. God was still active in his pursuit of Daniel's heart.

Does this not reveal the power of parents united in agreement to pray and plead with God on behalf of their child? I must admit, though I prayed, I did not expect this kind of unleashed power. Looking back, I wonder why we did not continue to pray with the same force each day.

A Few More Words Just for You

1. Do you know a family doing their best to raise their rebellious teen? Come alongside them, support and love them. Love their teen. Do not approach them in a spirit of judgement or condemnation. If you have some wisdom to offer or insight into the situation, please share, but always in a spirit of love.

2. Open the eyes of your spiritual heart and see what we missed. God hears, and he answers faith-filled, power-packed prayers, specifically and tangibly. Persist and seek him with all your heart.

Some days it's difficult to know just
what to do.

Taking a Stand

9

As the school year was coming to an end, my conviction to move away was stronger than ever. The conversations between Gary and me grew stressful. "Gary, do you see what is happening? These kids will not back down. They are determined to suck our son into their culture. We need to get out of here!" I pleaded with him to come around to my way of thinking.

"Susie, I think we need to wait on God."

"No! God says we are to take care of our family first. He's made that clear. Please, think about what I am saying."

Gary seemed physically weighed down by the current circumstances with Daniel and my insistence that we move. He had no answer. He processes slowly, but I had already determined it was dangerous to wait any longer. It seemed there was no resolution to our situation. I felt abandoned by my husband.

One day I reached my limit and couldn't take any more delay. I told my husband that I would not stay and watch my son be swallowed up in the sins of this city. My emotions were volitile. I felt desperate. "Gary, I do not believe God wants us to remain in this town and lose our child! God gave us children as a trust. We are to protect them. If we cannot protect Daniel here, we need to move and move quickly!"

My words confused and hurt Gary. I know he was struggling between the obvious danger to our son and his belief that God had called him to this city. It was the first time in years the church had experienced growth. He was praying God would show up, right where we lived.

I had never come against my husband like this before and have never since. But I took a stand. I announced that I would not stay. I made plans to move to the safest place I knew in Hudsonville, Michigan. Very dear friends of ours took Daniel in while we made preparations to move.

We told Daniel we were going to visit our friends in Michigan. Joel was Daniel's little childhood buddy and Daniel loved this family, but he was in such an irritated state that he refused to go.

I tried again. "Daniel, come on. The kids want to see you. They are so excited we are coming."

Up until the last minute, we did not know if he'd get into the car. I packed a suitcase full of his things and hid it in the trunk. We were relieved when he reluctanly climbed into the back seat.

We stayed beyond the weekend and on Monday enrolled Daniel in the high school where two of the Nickerson kids attended. Joel and Jody kept their eyes on Daniel. They were protective and made sure he kept himself in line. He skipped school once. The Nickersons gave him outside chores as a consequence and were impressed by how vigorously he completed them.

A couple of months after Daniel's move, I temporarily moved in, too, while searching for housing, obtaining employment, and making arrangements for school for all three children.

I found a cute little yellow house in Hudsonville. Though it was small, it would be just right for our family. I called Gary and he agreed to put in an offer. The offer went through and within a couple of weeks, we were nestled into our new home.

I obtained employment in human resources through a local hospital. Gary visited every week as he, too, searched for employment. After he found a job as a painter, he joined us in Hudsonville. For months he travelled on the weekends from Michigan to Illnois and back again. He cared about our church and did not want to leave our dear folks there without a pastor.

I share this part of the journey to give you a true account of what took place. But in sharing, I need to confess that my approach to my husband was not God honoring. In retrospect, I wish I would have been softer. I was sick with worry and running scared. I had approached Gary over and over, but I felt like he did not hear me.

I wish, in that last plea, I had presented the move with a greater respect for his position. I pretty much said, "You stay; I'm not! I'm out of here, like it or not!"

There are always what-ifs when you feel you've blown

it: What if I had gently approached him and stated I cannot continue as we are? What if I had pulled in the support of a counselor to help us sort it through? What if . . .?

God brought conviction to my heart just recently. He revealed to me that I had overstepped my God-given role to respect my husband in his leadership position. I grieved my attitudes and apologized to him. He hugged me close and said, "I love you!"

Thankfully, God's grace covers me and I rest in his promise. "And we know that for those who love God all things work together for good, for those who are called according to his purpose" (Rom. 8:28). "All things" includes our sins and our mistakes. His grace covers it all.

A Few More Words Just for You

1. When you feel pushed against a wall and you cannot take any more, get someone to advocate for you. One who will help you be heard and help you hear your partner's voice.

2. Though your world is spinning, keep your God ordained role in place. "However, let each one of you love his wife as himself, and let the wife see that she respects her husband." Ephesians 5:33

Hope for a Fresh Start

10

Not long after our move to Michigan, Gary began to see the situation with more clarity. He apologized for not stepping up and taking the lead. He admitted that he did not see the depth of devastation and danger surrounding our family until after we got out of Utica. His words were like a balm to my soul.

Another insight came soon after our move. In a conversation with my oldest daughter, I learned that she, too, was in trouble. Renee approached me with a hug as she said, "Mom, I'm really glad you guys moved us here."

"You are?" I asked.

"Yes. I was following Daniel and was about to join him and his friends."

My heart seemed to drop into the pit of my stomach as I considered the close call. Soon my heart sang as I contemplated the deliverance God had provided.

Early on in our new town, Daniel said, "This town is pretty clean. Do you know the best kids in Utica are like the worst kids in Hudsonville?" Amazing insight and affirming words to this mama's heart. Both of my oldest children expressed deep appreciation that we had started over in a new place for our family's sake.

The decision to live in this little town proved to be a wise choice, which kept Daniel away from a broader array of opportunities toward destruction. Here Daniel couldn't buy cigarettes, and alcohol was not available for sale. Yet our son continued to display rebellious attitudes.

A Few More Words Just for You

1. Even when your course of action appears to have removed the fertile environment for rebellion, keep your guard up, your eyes open, and your heart in prayer, for rebellion springs from the heart.

The heart is deceitful above all things, and
desperately sick; who can understand it?
Jeremiah 17:9 (ESV)

Upsurge in Rebellion

11

D r. Warren had warned us to brace for some horrific years ahead. He also encouraged us that he was certain our son would "someday" come around and break out of his rebellion. As I waited through many years, I counted on Dr. Warren's words.

Daniel showed up his first day at school with his bangs covering one eye and his hat worn backwards—a sign of rebellion in the small town we had moved from. Some of the teens in Hudsonville who thought of Daniel as some kind of an icon mimicked this style. (My apologies to all the parents of kids he influenced.)

As the school year progressed, I watched his behavior follow the same previous downward spiral. It was happening again. He skipped school, pushed the curfew, exploded when given any type of direction. He bragged about all-night rides with gang members. He smoked and drank alcohol and associated with dark characters, even disappearing for days.

Gary and I joined a Tough Love group that met once a week. The group helped us establish firm boundaries. Still Daniel continued to break every rule. I was frantic, and in my desperation I pooled together several resources, including books on parenting and rebellion, phone numbers to our Tough Love group, and a professional counselor who is also a pastor's wife. I counted heavily on my friends. God gave me four kindred-heart friends for such a time as this. Each one spoke truth and helped me with last minute strategies

I thought I could control the situations my son's behaviors created. When his anger erupted, I pointed to the door and told him to take a walk, cool off, and come back when he could manage his mouth.

One time when he brought his sketchy friends to our house, Renee called me. "Mom, Daniel brought these crazy-looking guys into the house. What do I do?"

"Renee, don't panic. Get your brother aside and tell him Mom said to leave with his friends. Tell him he is not allowed to bring anyone over when we are not home." I directed Renee to call the police if he refused.

He left, but not before one of his friends stole food from our freezer.

Our Tough Love group helped us navigate his determination to break all of our house rules. He broke curfews, he refused to get up for school many mornings, he pushed the language rules by inserting curse words into angry conversations. We met each violation with a consequence.

Though outwardly we were keeping order, the chaos was affecting my health and emotions. It was destroying the peace and sanctity of our home.

I kept believing that "This can't go on forever. We'll get

over this hump and he'll start thinking straight." We invested so much in his life. We sent him to Heartlight, we took him to counseling, we practiced patience, we prayed—surely there would be a pay-off.

I kept thinking, I can fix this! I was intelligent (my college major was social psychology), I was resourceful, and I had many connections. I also thought I had a bit of my own wisdom to draw upon. (Notice the use of "I"?) But nothing worked! Rebellion was gobbling up my boy. Nothing I did, nothing I said worked. Absolutely nothing! My son was out of control.

I viewed Daniel's life like he was recklessly speeding down a dangerous road where evil and destruction lurked. I feared for his life, while he feared nothing! Many nights I went to bed scared because I had no clue where he was.

A Few More Words Just for You

1. Establish and keep firm boundaries, being consistant with household rules. Your rebel will push until he finds the door closed. At some point he will respect you for placing firm boundaries.

2. Do not think you can fix your rebel. Only God can reach into a heart and change it.

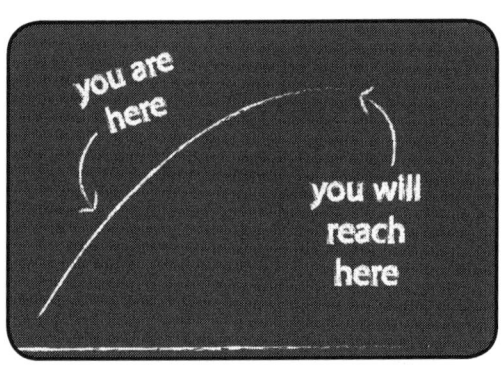

Do not conform to the pattern of this world, but be transformed by the renewing of your mind. Then you will be able to test and approve what God's will is—his good, pleasing and perfect will.

Romans 12:2 (ESV)

Coping

12

The drive to my job each day took thirty minutes. Alone in the car and away from the eyes of my girls, I let my pent-up emotions burst. I grieved and cried and prayed all the way to work.

Turning into the parking lot, I'd pull myself together and work like a crazy woman all day long, only to collapse in my car and sob most of the way back home. Many days, I drove past my exit and found myself thirty minutes beyond it before I realized where I was. Such was my distress.

Returning home from work, I'd pull myself together and with a prayer for strength put on my happy face for the sakes of my girls and husband.

During these drives, whenever I saw a teenager walking the streets and carrying a backpack, tears filled my eyes and multiplied as excruciating pain stabbed at my stomach. My heart cried out as I prayed for the lost teen as well as his mother. I was utterly broken. The pain was unbearable, but somehow I kept moving forward doing everything in my power and strength to try to fix Daniel.

I talked to him, I pleaded and reasoned with him, but

he would not listen.

I had tunnel vision. When I wasn't at work, all I could think about was how to help Daniel. I was obsessing. I did not apply or process the well-known phrase Let Go and Let God. I still had a fight ahead of me. It was a fight God would win.

A Few More Words Just for You

1. Identify your obsessive thoughts. Recognise that obsessive thinking is unhealthy and in no way will help your rebelling child. Stop obsessing.

2. God goes places we cannot. He is able to protect and reach into the heart of your child. Practice releasing your teen to God. Tell God you trust him to work in your child's heart

How Can This Be?   13

The emotional roller coaster was taking its toll. The struggles of my heart were surfacing. I developed some autoimmune disorders, and extreme exhaustion became a way of life. At work, I'd drink coffee all day long just to keep my head up and off the desk.

I kept looking back on our lives, trying to tear it apart and discover what I had done to contribute to Daniel's rebellion. Although I was blaming myself, I had trouble pinpointing what I had done wrong.

My husband and I had poured ourselves into teaching all of our children God's ways. We encouraged and worked with them to memorize scriptures because we believed that God's Word implanted in the heart would guide them and be with them forever.

One day my youngest daughter, a young teen, approached me as I sat on our front porch in a world of pain. Feeling vulnerable I said, "All I ever wanted was a safe home for my children."

"Mom, you have provided a safe place for us, and we do know we are loved," Christy said.

Her words lifted my sight beyond the situation with Daniel to the perception of one of my other children. This declaration imparted a much-needed rest to my soul.

On another day, Christy walked in on me sitting in a pool of tears. She sat beside me silently for quite a while. Then she said, "Mom, when I grow up, I want to be just like you."

I pulled her toward me and held her tight. Oh, how I needed to hear those words from my child. Though she may not understand the ways she lifted me, Christy's tender heart ministered to me time and time again.

As I considered our days dealing with rebellion and applying consequences for unacceptable behavior, I realized that my husband and I had worked hard at disciplining in love. Did we fail? You betcha. Did we strive to be consistent? Yes, we did.

I was sure that I had laid a foundation of love. So how could this happen when love covered my son? I was in tune with my children's needs. If I sensed unrest or anger in them, I got down on their level, looked them in the eyes, and said, "Do you need your love cup filled?" Invariably they would answer, "Yes!" and fall into my arms.

Connecting with each of my kids was a priority, and making deliberate decisions to develop a deep bond of trust was paramount to me. I practiced listening to them without interruption. I helped them to draw sound conclusions by asking the right questions. I then supported their decisions.

When my girls came in after a date, they often jumped

into my bed and shared every detail. Although I had to be at work early the next day, my sleep was not as important as the intimacy built in those late hours.

I invested my time, energy, and heart to provide a safe place for our children to thrive. Our home was the gathering place for my kids' friends. I was once called the Kool-Aid mom. I'd much rather have my kids at our house than at someone else's. Their teen friends called me Mom and often invited me to join them in our family room to hang out with them.

Although I am not perfect, and my husband would freely admit that he is not either, our home was a pretty good picture of stability. How could this craziness have happened? Somehow I believed that raising my kids in a stable Christian home was a guarantee that they would breeze through life unscathed by the world. How wrong I was! I had failed to consider that Daniel's free will, his living in a sin-cursed earth, and his human nature affected how he responded to life and the temptations it produced.

When that truth hit me, I found a level of relief. I did not have to carry all the responsibility of my son's choices and behavior.

A Few More Words Just for You

1. Invest in your kids. Take extra measures to connect with them.

2. Remember that your teen has a free will and may chose to go his or her own way.

3. Never give up on your rebel. Remember, God will do what you cannot do.

God in the Midst

14

The turmoil and pain that filled our days clouded my perspective. Daniel's outbursts and the ensuing disruption to our family had the potential to take me down. I say "potential" because God stepped into my mess time and time again.

On many occasions God spoke very personally and individually to me. He gave me hope and let me know that he was near and very much involved in our lives. On one occasion God revealed himself to me as Jehovah Jirah, God Provides.

After our move to Hudsonville, as we were settling in our new town and trying to adjust, finances became a challenge. Gary and I both had changed jobs and were making considerably less than we had before the move. One Sunday afternoon, as I was trying to plan a meal, I realized I needed some ingredients. I did not have the money to buy them, so I rumaged through the cupboards looking for other options. I came up empty and had no clue what to make for dinner.

The stress was stretching me beyond my ability to cope.

I went to my bedroom and stuffed my face in a pillow and sobbed, not wanting anyone but God to hear me. I prayed and asked God to show me in some small way that he cared about me, about our family, and that he had not abandoned me. As I lay on my bed, listening for his still small voice, I heard a knock at our front door. Soon after, Gary came into my room. "We have a visitor, honey."

I dried my tears and checked the mirror before meeting our guest. As I rounded the corner, I saw our pastor standing by the door, holding bags of groceries. I perceived him as an angel from God bearing witness to the fact God hears and he answers prayer. Chills ran down my spine as gratitude filled my heart with joy.

Another time God very specifically answered my prayer was one day while I was agonizing over my son. After a lively confrontation with Daniel, which ended with his stomping off to his room and slamming the door, I felt desperation and panic rising within. I fell to the kitchen floor and sobbed. I prayed, "Dear God, your Word tells me that you are the potter and I am the clay, but the heat of this furnace is unbearable, I can't take it anymore. Have you forgotten about me? Do you see me? I am melting away in the fire of affliction. I feel all alone."

My prayer turned to a request. "Dear Father, my son needs other people to reach out to him; he needs a Christian friend to take him under their wing and show him unconditional love. It seems he, too, is alone in this battle."

I cannot recall how long I lay there as the light of God's

presence ministered to me, but suddenly I was stirred into the present by a knock at the door. I answered the door to see Joel, Daniel's childhood friend. "Howdy, Mrs. Ream. How are you?" Joel grabbed me up in a big hug.

"I'm okay, Joel," I said, wondering about his visit.

"Where's Daniel?" he asked.

"Upstairs in his bedroom."

Joel sprinted up the stairs, taking the steps two at a time, and soon appeared back downstairs with Daniel. As they headed toward the front door, Joel said, "Dan and I are going to McDonald's. We'll be back soon."

I was humbled and very aware of God's targeted answers to my heart's cry.

Hope once more lifted me. I could face another day.

A Few More Words Just for You

1. Keep going to God. Ask him to show up for you and your rebel.

2. Be honest in your prayers. God already knows your heart.

3. Thank God when he answers your prayers. Never forget his faithfulness to you!

If any of you lacks wisdom, let him ask God, who gives generously to all without reproach, and it will be given him. But let him ask in faith, with no doubting, for the one who doubts is like a wave of the sea that is driven and tossed by the wind.

James 1:5-6 (ESV)

The Games He Played

15

Gary and I once again sought Christian counseling to help us navigate our way through this mess. We changed counselors several times, learning that just because a counseling office advertises it is Christian does not make it so.

In one of our sessions, the counselor nailed Gary. The counselor's words helped Gary to see how futile his actions were when reacting to Daniel's rebellious words. "Gary, you have to stop biting every time Daniel throws out the bait." He positioned his hands as if he were holding a fishing rod. Then he cast the imaginary line out across the room. "Do you see it, Gary? Your son is baiting you. He is looking for a fight, and he knows what bait to use to get you to bite. Don't bite!"

It would not have been wrong for Gary to be firm and deal with Daniel's disrespect and out of control behavior. But he reacted. He could not keep his temper under control. The 'don't bite,' method worked as he practiced self-control, remaining calm and unphased.

I began to see this bait-casting pattern in Daniel's behavior. He was playing games with us. He deliberatly set us up to get us to react. For example, my husband came to me one day, concern etched on his face. "Susie, I can't find my shoe. One shoe is in the closet. I've searched high and low. It's like the other one vanished."

As Gary was speaking, I caught a smirk curling my son's mouth. I turned to Daniel. "Daniel, do you know anything about Dad's shoes?"

His smirk turned to feigned innocence. "How would I know where Dad's shoe is? Even if I did know, why would I tell you?"

There it was. He had just cast the line. I shot my husband a look that said, "Do not react!" Moving beyond my son's earshot, I whispered, "He's looking for a fight. Don't satisfy him."

Following my advice, Gary went to his room and put on another pair of shoes. Before he left, Daniel showed up holding Gary's missing shoe. "Look what I just found." His game-playing smile stretched across his face.

Gary's shoulders sagged as he looked at me. He shook his head as if to say, "I can't believe the audacity of this kid."

I smiled and signaled with upraised eyebrows. "Please don't react."

Gary took his shoe from Daniel, went upstairs, and changed into these shoes. Daniel did not get satisfaction for his game playing, at least not this time.

Gary had a very hard time withholding his anger when

Daniel played games like this. This situation could have escalated into a huge scene, which would have disrupted the whole house.

A Few More Words Just for You

1. Take your time when searching for a Christian counselor. You don't have to settle on the first one you meet.

2. Learn the wisdom of not reacting to your rebel's taunts. Don't bite every time your child casts the bait or pushes your buttons.

Better is open rebuke
than hidden love.
Faithful are the wounds of a
friend; profuse are the kisses of
an enemy.
Proverbs 27:5-6

16

Boundries

One thing I knew deep in my heart was that I could not allow the unacceptable behaviors of teenage rebellion to slip by unnoticed. If I were to accept them without consequence, my son would surely push it to a new level. I was very firm with my boundaries. Swearing or verbally attacking a family member was not acceptable in our home.

Daniel was allowed to express his anger and even raise his voice if he needed to release those destructive emotions. When he violated the boundary, I pointed to the door and said firmly, "Take a walk. Cool down and don't come back until you can control your words and actions."

Although, at the time, these boundaries did nothing to prevent his repeated, headlong leap into destruction, it provided a sense of normalcy for our girls. Years later those limits paid off big-time. Our son told us that the boundaries provided a sense of stability to his heart. He thanked us for putting the limits in place, saying that he does not know where he would be today if we had not established our boundaries.

One such boundary was the curfew we set for Daniel. When we said 11:00 p.m., we meant it. One night he showed up at 11:05. Oh, how it killed me when he came to the glass door, knocking and asking to be let in! Trust me, with every fiber of my being I wanted to let my boy in, but I knew his heart. If I let him come in after curfew just one time, he would continue to push the limits.

That night, looking into his face, I said, "No, son, you may not come in. You are late."

His eyes and posture communicated humiliating rejection. He turned away from me and walked out to the road in front of our house. I watched him walk into the street and, to my horror, lay down. I felt panic rising inside as I struggled to process his actions. I immediately called our Tough Love sponsor and blurted the scenario so fast I am amazed he understood me.

A soft chuckle came from the other end of the line. "Susan," he began. "You have two options. You can either call the police and tell them your son is lying in the middle of the road, or you can go to bed. I assure you, if a car comes, he will get up. He's manipulating you."

"Really?" His insight astonished me.

Although this possibility seemed inconceivable, I trusted this man. In the end, it turned out to be an epiphany for me. Once again, my naïvety was exposed. I never considered that Daniel was deliberately manipulating me, but in time I learned that he most certainly was.

That night I went to bed with fear clutching at my throat and tears rolling down my face. I begged God to take over. After a fitful night, I awoke early in the morning, my stomach tied in knots. I walked to the front door and peered out. Daniel was curled up in our little three feet by four feet breezeway. How do you spell that kind of relief? I smiled and opened the door. "Would you like to come in now?"

He nodded yes and very humbly shuffled in, took a shower, and went to school.

A Few More Words Just for You

1. Allow your child to express his frustraton and pent-up emotions. But put conditions around his expression. No swearing, no tearing anyone down, no hitting the wall, etc. If your teen violates the condition, point to the door and say, "Leave! You can come back when you cool down."

2. Do not allow your rebel to control your household. If you do not set boundaries, you will become codependant. Your child will get increasingly savvy at manipulation. You harm your child and enable him when you give in to his bullying or ignore his unacceptable behavior.

For this reason I remind you to fan into flame the gift of God, which is in you through the laying on of my hands, for God gave us a spirit not of fear but of power and love and self-control.
2 Timothy 1:6-7 (ESV)

More Lessons for Mom

17

God had many lessons to teach me about being a parent to a rebel. God confronted me on the issue of the dynamic between Daniel and me when his anger escalated.

Back then I could be pretty feisty, and if you could dish it out, I could serve it right back. My confrontational behavior manifested when Daniel was in one of his defiant rages exhibiting out-of-control behavior.

After telling Daniel that he was not to go to his girlfriend's house when her mother was gone, he began pacing and raged at me. "I am sixteen years old. You can't tell me what to do anymore! You have no control over my life. I make my own decisions, and I will live my life the way I want to!"

I gave it right back to him. "You, young man, are still living under our roof! As long as you are living here, you will respect our rules! You will lower your voice and stop creating chaos in this house. Do you understand me?"

I spoke louder than him, so he raised his voice until it boomed. "You have no control over me. Do you understand me?"

His flagrant display of disrespect set me off. "How dare you talk to your mother this way!"

There came a day when my faithful Father spoke very pointedly to my heart. He revealed that this argumentative, confrontational style of communication served only to create an atmosphere of instability. The situation always spun out of control. Daniel's anger escalated when I challenged him. It accomplished nothing good and never provided any resolution.

As I stood toe-to-toe with my son one day, God spoke in a still small voice. He said something like, "Well, Susie, how's this working for you?" God whispered, "Conducting a hollering match is not beneficial to him." I am always humbled and a bit stunned when I "hear" his voice.

As a parent, my job is to seek to understand my child and do whatever it takes to help him, not to harm him. After God spoke, I determined to change the dance. The next time Daniel flew into a rage (in those days I didn't have to wait very long), with God's help, I remained calm and quiet. I looked deep into his eyes and listened attentively. What followed astounded me. As I stood quietly, his defiant, oppositional fury reversed and gradually decreased to a level where we could talk. That day I began to understand that my self-control was one of the keys to helping my son. I held that key.

It became evident that when his world was crashing around him, my son desperately needed to know that I was stable and in control of myself. This truth turned out to be the saving grace that kept our relationship intact even as my son's world continued to spiral down.

A Few More Words Just for You

1. When your child's world is spinning out of control, he desperately needs you to remain stable and self-controlled.

2. God speaks in a still small voice. If you're not attentive, you will miss his message.

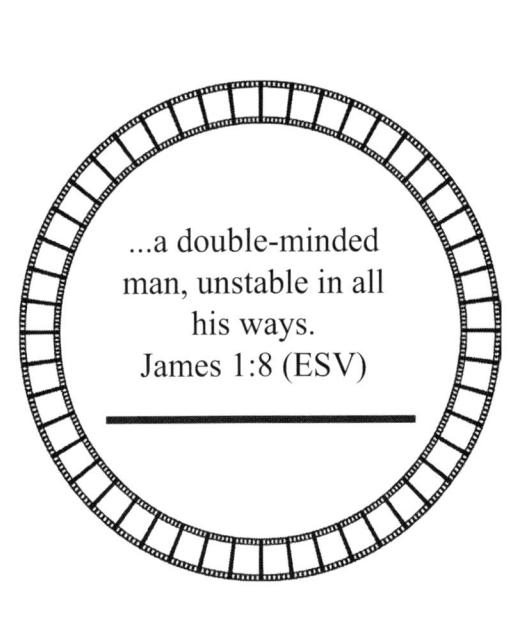

...a double-minded
man, unstable in all
his ways.
James 1:8 (ESV)

He Crossed the Line 18

There came a time when I had to switch gears because the situation called for an in-your-face approach. Daniel was fifteen years old and caught up in one of his power trips. His anger was raging out of control. He knew how to trip his dad's trigger, and he was doing a good job of it. "I'm out of here, and I'm not coming back!" Daniel screamed.

"You are to come home and be in by eleven p.m." his father roared back.

Daniel's eyes filled with hot anger. "You are not my boss! I will do whatever I want to do!"

Gary was hot too. "You are my son, and you will do whatever I tell you to do! Your belligerent behavior is unacceptable. You need to back off. Now!" Scorching indignation accompanied Gary's words.

In his fury Daniel turned to his father and picked up a knife. "I am going to kill you!"

I knew this threat could not stand unchallenged. Before his dad could say a word, I rallied every ounce of courage and stared Daniel straight in the eyes. "Daniel! You get upstairs, and you will pack your bags and get out now! You will never, ever threaten a member of this family! Never! Do you understand me?"

He stared back at me through blank eyes. Then he hung his head, went upstairs, packed his bags. Within minutes he was gone. It hurt to watch him walk out that door. I cried my heart out to God, asking him to protect my son. I knew beyond a shadow of a doubt that if I had let his threat stand, he would have felt the power to bully and destroy. I am confident my reaction was merited. In this situation, an in-your-face response was appropriate. My son never threatened a family member again.

A Few More Words Just for You

1. Know when to be quiet and listen attentively and when to take a strong stance against abuse.

2. Never allow your rebel to threaten a family member.

Hound of Heaven

19

After Daniel had left our home, God pursued him. Like the "Hound of Heaven," God chased him down. Daniel was never really alone.

Years later, Daniel shared several instances that highlight God's presence with him. One of his stories stressed the Enemy's influence. Daniel told me about a day he was sitting in McDonald's, drinking some cocoa and trying to get warm. A lady approached him and said, "Son, are you in trouble?"

He wondered why she had singled him out. "No, I'm fine."

She then went on to tell him that evil spirits were all around him. Talk about terrifying! That was one moment he wished he could have denied her claims, but he could not shake the feeling of evil following him.

One of the persistent prayers of my heart in those years was "God, please send believers into my son's life. He won't listen to us, but you have servants everywhere. Let them speak your truth into Daniel's life."

In answer to my prayers, Daniel told me he couldn't go anywhere without Christians being there, waiting to talk to him about Jesus and his love. "I go to work, and Tony asks me if I know how much God loves me. I run into an old classmate, and he tells me God captured his heart and now he is in full-time ministry."

God's involvement in my son's life and his answers to my prayers helped us to stay the course and never give up!

Another one of my prayers asked God to discipline Daniel when he stepped out of line. I prayed that if he did something wrong, he would get caught. And he did, all the time—by the police, the school, in stores, and at work. On one occasion Daniel ran his car over a curb and plowed into someone's boat. He took off to escape punishment. We learned about the incident and called the police—we were never bail-you-out parents. To this day, he does not know we turned him in. If he reads this book, he will know.

Daniel got kicked out of school for starting a fight and pinning a kid against the locker. Sometime after he was expelled, the superintendent of schools contacted us to tell us about an incident we were unaware of. After being kicked out, Daniel met with this superintendent of schools and said, "I am sorry for all the trouble I have made throughout my high school years. Thank you for your patience and for kicking me out. I deserved it." Even in the midst of rebellion, Daniel retained his sense of justice. This man was proud of my son. Imagine that!

One time he stole cigarettes from the store. He got caught and was banned from ever entering that store again. Another time, out of anger and frustration, he said, "Mom, would you please stop praying I get caught. I can't get away with anything!"

I smiled and sent up a "Thank you, Lord." Not the reaction he was looking for, but he couldn't keep himself from smiling back at me.

A Few More Words Just for You

1. Pray that God chases your rebel down, and that he sends believers to speak into your rebel's life

2. Never bail your rebellious child out of trouble. If you do, you remove the penalty for his or her actions and the opportunity to learn from mistakes. If you rescue your child, you create codependency, which creates weak adults who never own their own messes

.

3. Pray your rebel gets caught when he chooses to sin. Pray he learns that when he chooses to sin, he chooses to suffer. Pray against the Enemy.

Doing It Backwards

20

Daniel started dating a girl from school not long after we moved to Hudsonville. The two of them consistantly fought our boundaries. We soon learned that his girlfriend and her siblings (all teens) were unsupervised most of the time. We found Daniel at her house time and time again. When we found him unsupervised at her home, we demanded he come home. One time, when I went to her house to bring him home, he glared at me. "No. I'm not going with you." He sat, staring at the television.

"Okay, that's fine with me." I answered. I sat down on the couch beside him, as if to make myself at home. Looking around I noted several other teens hanging out. The brother of Dan's girlfriend opened the refridgerator, searching for something to eat. I was disheartened to see only Diet Coke and butter. My heart hurt for these kids.

We sat for a few minutes before Daniel got up, grabbed his shoes, and slowly laced them up. Standing up, he walked to the door. I followed him out and we drove home.

He had been dating his girlfriend for about a year when we learned that they were expecting a baby. (Only after their second child was born would they marry.)

These two baby girls became the bright spot in our darkest days. Such happiness and beauty came from the innocence of their lives. I was Nana and they were my grandgirls. Who knew such joy could be birthed out of such tribulation?

My daughters adored their neices. Renee bought them tons of clothes. Christy and Renee took turns caring for the girls. We all loved on them. Years later, when his girlfriend became his wife, she told me that she learned how to be a mother by watching Renee and me with her girls.

Though Daniel was married, he continued to live life without caution.

A Few More Words Just for You

1. Look for the silver lining in the dark clouds. Sometimes in the middle of heartache you will find a blessing. Children are always a blessing from the Lord.

God Stepped In

21

Coping with my rebellious teenaged son turned out to be way too much for me. Though I went through many episodes of releasing him to God, I kept taking the burden and responsibility back. It took many, many years, at least ten, before I finally collapsed in despair and realized I could do nothing to help my son.

That truth knocked me to the ground. I cried out to God. "Help me! Please, reach and rescue my boy, my only son, the son whom I love more than life itself. I have no other place to turn. I can't do it anymore." I finally came to the end of myself, and that is when God stepped in.

I kept order and maintained peace within the walls of my house by implementing firm boundaries, but I could not make my son better. When I finally gave up trying to control the situation, God peeled back my hold on Daniel, one white-knuckled, death-gripped finger at a time, and released my control over my son.

In answer to my prayer and my desparate plea for God

to take over, something miraculous and totally unbelievable happened. The only way I know to explain it is by saying that it felt like God cut the umbilical cord between my son and me. I could no longer feel pain or even a connection to him. It was disturbing, to say the least, but also exactly what I needed to survive. God's intervention saved my emotional and physical well-being. God did it. I could never have backed away on my own.

As God intervened and I released my son to his care, taking my hands off completely, I witnessed miracles happening in Daniel's life. He went back to church where the preaching of the Word touched and influenced him. Daniel loved Pastor Duane. Gary and I and his sister Renee and family joined him for a season to support him. We were all celebrating his return to the church. Pastor Duane was loving, kind, wise, and one of the best expositors we've ever heard. Daniel was drawn to a church preaching the Word without apology.

I continued to pray, and God answered those prayers by surrounding Daniel with believers who seemed to be coming out of the woodwork. All through his days of rebellion, God sent believers who boldly spoke into his life. Daniel himself was well aware that the Hound of Heaven was chasing him down.

In the early years of his first marriage, he and his wife moved next door to a strong believer. Scott became one of my son's best friends. Whenever Daniel was on one of his highs, thinking he was king of the world, Scott would shoot him down and bring him back to reality. Conversations like, "Dan, you can't be going around talking like you own the world and everyone should bow to you. You have a family that needs you to love them, and they need your stability." Daniel listened to his friend, and he respected him.

Tim lived in Daniel's apartment complex, and the two became friends. Tim was the voice of reason in my son's life. He spoke words of wisdom into his chaos time and time again.

In place of panic and despair, I now felt consumed by God's love as I witnessed his pursuit of my son. Reflecting back on all of the ways that God worked to reach and restore Daniel, I am in awe. Right in the midst of the mess, God built faith into my life.

A Few More Words Just for You

1. Do not carry the weight that is intended for God. It will ruin your health and take a huge toll on your emotions.

2. Stop trying to fix your child. Only God can work in a rebel's heart.

3. God's power is released when you turn the control over to him. God will reach your child at the heart level. He can do what you cannot.

4. Never lose hope. Remember, there is a God in heaven

who loves your boy or girl far more than you are capable of loving or understanding.

5. Pray and release. As you pray, trust God. He is at work!

For God so loved the world, that he gave
his only Son, that whoever believes in him
should not perish but have eternal life.
John 3:16 (ESV)

My Son Restored

22

After more than twenty years of coping with a rebellious son, I have a grown son who makes me very proud. He has come back to his roots, and he loves God. Daniel is not perfect, but he holds a heart full of wisdom, compassion, and love.

When I look at my son today, I am filled with pure joy. My heart is filled with gratitude to Father God. The pain is all gone, and only a shadow of memories remain about lessons learned and of a God who works in the midst of every circumstance.

It's a marvel to witness a young man—my son, his son—who is stable, loving, responsible, ingenious, handsome (oh yes, as his mom I can say that), and so much more than I could have ever dreamed. God is a God of the impossible. He worked in and through every heartache to create a heart that is mighty and unmovable.

Daniel's first marriage was obliterated. The end result was Daniel receiving full custody of his girls. I am so proud of the way he invested, protected, and provided for his children during this heartbreaking period of his life.

Daniel's three beautiful daughters are precious. They are intellegent and well-adjusted. They exhibit wisdom in their choices—this is nothing short of God's amazing grace. Let me offer a post from Daniel's Facebook page—his own words express his changed heart.

Daniel: Just wanted to take a moment to publicly thank my Mom and Dad for being the BEST parents that a kid could have ever had. I know I wasn't the best teen, but you guys loved me through all the stuff that I did. You always showed me unconditional love no matter what I did. I just want to let you know that I appreciate EVERYTHING! It did not go unnoticed. I look back on my childhood and have nothing but wonderful memories, even through the bad times, because of two people who put their kids first. If I can even be half the parent that you guys were, I will be doing great. Love you guys and Thank You for the way that you guys raised and loved me.

My Response: What a way to make your Mother Blubber!!! Son, thank you for honoring us. We were not perfect and never had all the answers, but God did. You are loved much more than you can imagine. God brought us through the hard times and we ALL grew. We are proud of you, son, and there's no one on earth that could take your place. Now, if I can get my big red puffy red eyes to go back to normal, maybe I can proof this later. Forever and always your Mother I'll be.

Gary's Response: I came upstairs and noticed your mother had been crying—then I read your post . . . I am equally proud of you and thankful for the lessons we are all learning. Even as a young child you had a heart for God and excellent "people skills." Thanks for sharing your heart. I couldn't be prouder. The best is yet to come. Love you— Dad.

A few years ago, God led our son to a kind and tenderhearted woman who became his wife. Jackie has blessed our whole family with her gracious and giving heart. She has been a huge stabilizing anchor in my son's life. We praise God for the gift of a caring woman for our son and a dear daughter-in-law to us.

A Few More Words Just for You

1. Stay the course, be consistent.

2. Trust the Lord! God will make a way when there seems to be no way.

daughter... and why...
Teacher any further?
as soon as Jesus heard the
that was spoken, He said to
the ruler of the synagogue, "Do not
be afraid; only *believe.*"
37 And He permitted no one to
follow Him except Peter, James,
and John the brother of James.
Then He came to the house of
of the synagogue, and
and those who

God Continues His Work 23

It is now five years later. I thought the book was complete and the good ending was in place. But then my son was baptized recently and gave his testimony. Daniel said, "What a mighty God we serve! No more double-mindedness for me. I'm all in!"

As Daniel was walking into the tank, the pastor asked him if he went by Dan or Daniel. Daniel said, "I have taken my birth name back. I am Daniel."

We had named our beloved son after Daniel of the Bible, who purposed in his heart that he would not defile himself, that he would bow to no one but Jehovah God.

Before they placed our son under the water, he explained that he had been brought up in a Christian home and was, in fact, a pastor's kid. He explained that he understood the gospel, but when he heard his pastor talk about the double-minded man, he recognised himself; he was that double-minded man. "Everything just clicked!" he exclaimed.

Daniel continued to explain his years as a prodigal and how he turned back to the Lord about six years prior. He said he's been doing his best to study and do what Jesus teaches, but he was trying and failing because he was doing it in his own strength.

He had never fully surrendered, never bent his knee. Two weeks prior to his baptism, he bent his knee and proclaimed, "Nothing has been the same." God is at work in my son in a huge way.

If you have a prodigal, know that this son of mine, who is first and foremost God's son, is forty-two years old. There is still time for your prodigal. Don't give up! God will answer your prayers. Let hope fill your heart.

My cup overflows with the deepest gratitude to a God who chased down my son and never gave up. Praises be to the Lord of Lords and the King of Kings.

A Few More Words Just for You

1. Never lose hope. Wait for the day your prodigal comes home, and anticipate the celebration that occurs in heaven and in your home.

2. Claim Romans 8:28: "And we know that for those who love God all things work together for good, for those who are called according to his purpose." He works everything (the good, the bad, and the ugly things) together for our good. Trust him!

Where is Dad?

24

You may be wondering where Daniel's dad was in all of this. First, this is a book from a mother's perspective, and yet I believe it is important for you to have an understanding of our backgrounds.

As stated at the beginning of the book, I was born into a very dysfunctional home. My father was addicted to anger, my mother was passive, and both were alcoholics. I never felt safe or loved during my childhood. I grew up in the middle of all kinds of craziness.

Gary was raised almost as an only child, being born ten years after his brother and eight years after his sister. His home was quiet and very controlled. He grew up feeling loved and safe. He never witnessed anything close to this kind of rebellion. His reactions to Daniel's rebellious episodes ranged from being stunned, speechless, outraged, and clueless.

Gary's anger often exploded at the audacity of our son's behavior. Daniel responded with profanity as he walked away in a rage while giving his father the finger. My imagination could not have visualized such a crude response from my child. Talk about crazy making. Those were the days.

Gary was lost in the parenting realm. I felt the weight of parenting Daniel alone. I rushed home from work each day, hoping to get there before Gary. I was constanly nervous about what would happen if I wasn't there to step between Gary and Daniel. I passed on outings with friends so I could be home to keep the peace.

Gary has apologized profusely for not knowing how to handle the situations that came up. He was not equipped, trained, or prepared to walk this walk. To be honest, it drove a wedge between us for many years, but our mutual faith and trust in God kept us looking to him. God was the glue that held us together during all the chaos.

As a couple, we have put time and effort into rebuilding those years of disillusionment and pain. Now that the storm has blown over, I thank God for the amount of peace we now experience as a couple. "So I will restore to you the years that the swarming locust has eaten" (Joel 2:25).

Gary has grown through the fire. I marvel at his patience and wisdom with our grandchildren. He has a restored relationship with Daniel. They share a mutual trust and admiration. Out of the fire came pure gold.

In retrospect, I wish Gary would have connected to some men who were strong in the area of parenting. I had four friends who constantly spoke into my life. Gary had no one. The Tough Love group was very helpful, and he picked up wisdom in our weekly meetings. How much better it would have been to have had some men walking beside him, men who listened, cared, and pointed the way to clarity.

A Few More Words Just for You

1. Be aware of your great need of godly counsel. Align yourself with people who are strong in the area of parenting, especially those navagating the teen years.

2. Find a Christian support group. Our group was called Tough Love. At the end of this book you will find other groups.

Afterword

25

I'd like to leave you with a few more insights I have learned from walking through the years of chaos. I realized some things after the fact, so I share them in hopes of helping you to avoid the pitfalls I fell into.

Be Present

One thing I deeply regret in retrospect is that so much of my emotional energy went into my son. I neglected to tune in to some critical moments in my girls' lives. Listen carefully, dear parent. I know life is crazy right now, but let me urge you to be present and in the moment. Teach your children—all of them. Don't forget that you are responsible for all your children.

It's easy to lose perspective when your rebellious teen strikes out and wreaks havoc in the home. Focus on the big picture. You have other family members who need you. You get only one chance to live those years with them. You don't want to lose years of their lives, do you?

I understand how hard it is. It's like these monsters

called panic, fear, confusion, and desperation take over, and all perspective gets lost in the mess. I have been told, by my youngest, that I was there for her, but I feel the loss. It was as if my head was disconnected at the time, and the stress load was so heavy that I don't remember a lot of the special moments of their teen years.

My oldest daughter felt the loss and carried a lot of responsibility. I grieve that and have asked her forgiveness, which she sweetly granted. Today, she and my youngest daughter are beautiful young women who are wonderfully well-adjusted—another glimpse of God's amazing grace.

Keep Balanced and Stop Obsessing

As one who knows, let me encourage you that you will make it through this trial, though I doubt you think you will. Keep yourself balanced as much as possible. Stop the cycle of obsessing. Replace your obsessive thoughts with scriptures that address your worry. Start with, "Trust in the Lord with all your heart, and do not lean on your own understanding. In all your ways acknowledge him, and he will make straight your paths." Proverbs 3:5-6. Say it out loud to overpower the obsessive thoughts.

Keep a Routine

Routine is vital to emotional stability. When one member of a family is in full-blown rebellion, it affects all of the others. Your family's emotional stability is at risk. Find ways to keep your family healthy and emotionally stable. Keep regular routines, for they provide a sense of normalcy in a family system. Keep a checklist for each member. Checking off chores offers a sense of accomplishment and order.

Have Fun

Plan fun vacations and events with your other children. We took two big family vacations during this time. It was not easy for me because my heart felt wracked with worry for the son we left behind. Though I was hurting, we needed to create good memories for the girls. The girls had a blast, and my husband experienced a much-needed break. They have very fond memories of the vacations, and I experienced some great moments when I released my cares and entered into the fun too.

Self Care is Vital

You, as a parent, need to watch out for your emotional stability. Take care of yourself and carve out time to develop your unique gifts and abilities. At the time all of this turmoil began, I had been accepted into a reputable school, taking a writing course. I was learning so much and growing as a writer. But I eventually quit my course work because the burden of living in such conflict was too much.

Looking back, I wish I would have pushed through and

kept up with the course. Investing in my God-given abilities was a healthy discipline. I encourage you to keep your gifts, interests, and abilities alive, no matter what.

Do not lose yourself in chaos. These are crucial years for you too, and you'll never get them back. Take time with friends and laugh as often as you can. God knows your frame and your need of refreshment. He has said, "A cheerful heart is good medicine, but a crushed spirit dries up the bones" (Prov. 17:22).

Invest in your Relationship with God

Spend time in his Word because God breathed life into it. He holds the key to your kid's future. He is the one who has the answers to all of life's mysteries. As you go about your days, keep your eyes on the Lord.

Do Not Give Up on Your Rebel

Don't forget that you must never give up on your rebel. My mother used to say, "Susie, it seems everyone has given up on Daniel. But you—you never give up." She made me smile, and she was right. I had raised this boy. I knew his heart and the potential he possessed. If he could get through this nightmare, I believed God would use it for his honor and glory.

Though your out-of-control child is going through a crazy time in his life, move forward!

Trust God – He is at Work

Even though I failed the test of completely trusting God with my rebellious teenager many times over, I take comfort in God's grace and his unabashed love for me. I rest in the promise that "he works all things together for our good." If never challenged, how do we grow in faith? Out of this nightmare, God brought forth some excellent fruit in all of our lives.

Blessings to each one of you who are wading through days of a life turned upside down by rebellion. To those who are barely hanging on and to those who have lost hope, I pray God has used my story to turn your eyes upon him and to know that he is at work, whether you see it or not.

Hang in there and wait on the Lord. Be faithful in the little things. You may not think it makes a difference, but it does. Your life speaks louder than your words.

God bless you, and may he open the eyes of your heart and give you hope and faith that only he can give.

One Day They Will All Come

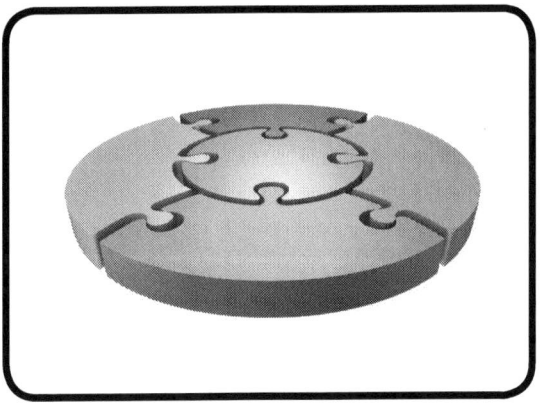

"...For the promise is for you and for your children and for all who are far off, everyone whom the Lord our God calls to himself."
Acts 2:39

A Pastor's Response 26

The situation Susan lived is not unique to many Christian parents, yet the rebellion of children can be the most soul-destroying, joy-sapping experience of any parent. Trying to raise children who will embrace personal faith can be one of the most difficult tasks for Christians. Scholars remain divided as to whether every Christian parent is promised household salvation. For many, myself included, that is our hope. Nevertheless, no matter how hard we seem to pray, the opposite too often happens. Instead of our children running to Jesus, they disappear into the distance, apparently exuberant to kick over the traces of Christianity.

Susan's story holds out hope that one day our children will embrace Jesus for themselves. One day, when they are born again, we will forget the labor pains of their rebellion. The most difficult spiritual discipline in waiting for this transformation is patience.

Yet the story of the prodigal son reminds us of this daily requirement. The father waited until the son came to his senses. Many of us would have hunted the son down, clipped the back of his ear, scolded him for his disobedience, and marched him back to our front door. However, the father was patient, incredibly so. The son had not only squandered his inheritance, ate with pigs, and became unfit for worship but had taken himself beyond the borders of Israel, to a place in religious folklore where God was rarely at work. Yet the father stood, patiently waiting. And then one day, as he stood gazing into the distant skyline, a small figure emerged. Daring to hope, he peered into the distance. Disheveled, his son had made it home. And I believe that one day our sons and daughters will return home, too.

Perhaps as a parent you are riddled with guilt, overcome by despair, and on the verge of a spiritual and emotional meltdown. Your heart heaves with a heaviness that is impossible to lift. You have no more tears to cry. You blame yourself for their wanderings. If only you had been a better parent. If only you had taught them more Scripture and prayed harder. If only you had resisted saying the things you said, then perhaps they would be serving God today. You rehearse daily everything that you would have done, but the disabling heartache is that the past cannot be reversed. Who needs the devil to remind you of your mistakes when you have perfected your own torture?

Let me reassure you and yet still be honest. It is quite likely that you have been part of the problem. Most parents are, for we are not perfect. Yet neither is any parent entirely responsible. Your precious son and dearly beloved daughter have for the time being made their own choices. The process of what they are going through may have been partially created by you, but the decision to walk it was theirs. However, with God there is always hope, and the hope is this: God loves them much more than we do, and, indeed, his love is much bigger than the mistakes we have made.

In the book of Ruth, Naomi encouraged Ruth to return home to worship pagan gods. Few of us have committed this offense. Yet God had greater plans for Ruth, plans that could not be thwarted by Naomi's poor judgment and inappropriate behavior. God never justifies our mistakes, but he can nullify them. Let go of the past and what you cannot change, and embrace the belief that God is in the process of changing you. With that same grace, one day God will change your child, too.

Perhaps you read Susan's story with a mix of pleasure and pain. In your better moments, you were happy with what God did in her family. In your worst moments, you were envious and heartbroken that the same spiritual recovery has not happened in your story. Having a child who hasn't turned his or her life over to God feels like living a persistent grief. Some days it feels even worse than the death of a loved one. At least such a death forces you into a period of adjustment. But how can you adjust to a child who has never embraced Christ?

I have worked with couples contending with infertility. They so desperately want to conceive. Many of these couples imagine holding not just any child but their child. They dress her for school, cheer when he graduates, and cry when they get married. It is often the power of our imaginations that brings us heartache and pain. Parents whose children have ignored God can cause a similar heartache. They find church a place of blessing and pain. They watch other children raise their hands in worship and wonder why it can't be theirs. They rejoice for parents whose children go on field mission trips and give their testimonies at the front of church, but still their heartache remains among a myriad of unanswered prayers. Susan's book brings joy and pain all in the same breath. Every day I breathe, I dream of a different world, a world in which all of my children are spiritually home.

The truth is that it hasn't happened yet, but I have not given up hope. As the early church gathered on the day of Pentecost, Peter addressed the expectant crowd. Referring to Joel, he made a bold declaration that the promise of the Holy Spirit was given not only to the covenant community but to their children, too. And whilst he claimed that this promise was to those who were afar off and open to all our Lord God calls, God thought it important enough to include such children as an entirely separate community to all the rest. Ponder this: God is thinking about our children in a particular way.

As a university student, I once heard a great philosopher. I travelled hundreds of miles to hear him. He was a convinced atheist and a compelling speaker. He was impressive and held the audience spellbound. Sadly, I was aware that he was the son of a Methodist minister. I can only imagine the nights his father stood at the city gate and longed for his own prodigal to return. This philosopher paraded his unbelief like an expensive garment. How ironic that as a lecturer, his week began by dismissing everything his father had said from the pulpit the previous day.

This irony remained with me for years, until one day as I was mulling over books in a well-known bookshop. One particular book caught my eye. The book's title was a defense for the existence of God, and under it, in bold letters, was the author's name. This man who once mocked the existence of God had surrendered his life to him. In old age, and not long before his own death, he had embraced the God he had so eloquently dismissed. The prodigal was indeed home. I am sure his earthly father would have rejoiced watching his son's transition, but, for whatever reason, God had other plans. Nevertheless, it happened, though not in the timescale his parents would have preferred.

I suppose that's the great hope—that one day our children will come. It might not be today, tomorrow, or even in your lifetime. However, the annals of history and the promise of the covenant reveal that often they do. You may have to whisper a petition for their salvation in your dying breath, but God is still listening. Perhaps long after people lay flowers on your grave, that rebellious child will find his or her way home. Do I lament the fact that I may not be around to see my children return? As long as they do, what cause would I have to lament? An aging mother may have wished her son had not been a thief. Why could her son have not been a reader in the synagogue like all the good children? Did she even hear his request to be remembered by

Jesus when he came into his kingdom? She didn't need to, for most likely she or others prayed that he would embrace God, and in his dying breath, nailed to a cross beside Jesus, he did. True, one thief remained obstinate, but let's cling to the observation that if you teach a child in the way he or she should go, when they are old they will not depart from it. When, perhaps, they are too old for you to be aware of their return. But age and the passing of years did not negate your tearful petitions and divinely implanted longings that your child would embrace the Savior. Why would you lament just when they come, rather than celebrate in hope and anticipation that they will one day come? And guess what? God will give you all eternity to celebrate it.

The problem with having children is that the labor pains carry on long after they are born. That is what it is like to live in a broken world. Nevertheless, I would rather feel the daily contractions of emotional pain today if, by God's grace, they were to culminate in my children's redemption tomorrow. The travail of raising children is often lifelong. But I plead with you continue to trust that it will end in their spiritual renewal. And one day we will look back from eternity's shore and witness their arrival. That day the suffering of our spiritual labor will subside as the echo and celebration of their conversion reverberates around the mansions of heaven. A mother perseveres through the pain if she believes that such a pain has a purpose. Likewise, I would find it difficult to believe that our loving God would subject us to such travail if our fervent pleading were not heard. That is our comfort and hope.

I, like many, am a recovering addict. My substance is not alcohol, illicit drugs, or pornography. Although it causes just as much pain and dysfunction, its name is Rebellion. It is one of the oldest and hardest sins to conquer. It ensnares us in the most unlikely of places. We may not snort it in public, but we hide it in our hearts. On the worst days it manifests to family and stranger alike. We live in constant dread of its arrival, but when it does, we experience fleeting pleasure and a lifetime of regret.

Daniel, if you happen to read this book, I plead with you: learn to forgive yourself. Your head will tell you one thing and your heart another. You may sometimes doubt, but not often, that God has forgiven you. You may even believe this, though find it hard accept, that your parents have forgiven you, too. You will suspect, and indeed others have already told you, that your rebellion has been difficult to forgive. At times one person stares at you with disapproving eyes. They gaze at you from the bathroom mirror. The biggest enemy to complete forgiveness may indeed be you!

I wonder, do you have a family and do you love them? You may be insulted by this question. Your children may be sweet and wholesome—let's pray they remain so. But even if they didn't, if whatever reason they wandered into a world of sin, heartache, and pain, would you love them any less? I thought not. Your parents may have grieved the heartache you caused; they may even have shouted things in anger and frustration that hurt you, too. But when they cried themselves to sleep at night, those tears were the frustrations, impatience, and anger of loving someone so much that it actually hurt.

Just thank God that their tears have ended in joy. You are not the finished article yet. Every addict to rebellion will suffer the after tremors associated with the earthquake of human defiance. Nevertheless, you are closer to home than when you first started out, and your parents have had the joy watching you make your way home.

The story in this book is not over, certainly not for the Ream family. They will experience flashbacks of misery and endure brief skirmishes from an ugly past. The legacy of previous battles hit us at the most unexpected times. Like soldiers suffering from post-traumatic stress, the sights and sounds of battle are never far away. Nevertheless, God remains faithful, and your ultimate victory has been secured. But other chapters still have to be written, and this book will never end. For contained within its pages is an eternal epilogue of unrelenting hope. For at the end of My Son His Son must be My Son Your Son. Every rebellious daughter and every strong-willed son could fill another page still to be written. Every wanton addict to a life without God will one day soon be the content of the next chapter. God has not forgotten you, dear parent, and, more important, he has not forgotten your child. Lay down your pen and propensity to write the next chapter, and let God tell the story of how he reached your wandering child.

Resources

Recommended Reading

Parenting Teens in a Confusing Culture, Mark Gregston, founder of Heartlight Ministries.

Shepherding a Child's Heart, Dr. Tedd Tripp, pastor of Grace Fellowship Church, Hazleton, Pennsylvania. I heard Paul and Tedd Tripp after Daniel was grown. I wish I'd had their resources available to me at the time. I am glad you do! Dr. Tripp focuses on addressing the root of issues (the heart) rather than just the outer behavior (symptoms).

Age of Opportunity, Dr. Paul David Tripp, president of Paul Tripp Ministries and Professor of Pastoral Life and Care at Redeemer Seminary, Dallas, Texas; Executive Director of the Center for Pastoral Life and Care, Fort Worth, Texas.

When I Lay My Isaac Down, Carol Kent, best-selling author and sought-after public speaker who weaves humor, hope, and faith into every presentation. Carol's only child is serving a life sentence in the state of Florida, and she is passionate about helping inmates and their families adjust to their "new normal." She and her husband, Gene, founded the nonprofit organization Speak Up for Hope, with the goal of helping inmates and their families through resources and encouragement.

Preparing for Adolesence, James Dobson, one of America's leading family psychologists. He is a wonderfully wise Christian counselor. Topics include avoiding feelings of inferiority, handling peer pressure, drug abuse, puberty, sexual development, menstruation, masturbation, romantic love, overcoming discouragement, sound decision making, and handling independence.

Recommended Websites

I discovered these after Daniel was grown. You will find in them lots of resources, helpful articles, and solid support.

BILY Because I Love You: Be sure to check out the Links and Resources. http://www.bily.org

The Total Transformation Program: Finally, a guaranteed, simple way to stop your child's defiant, out-of-control behavior . . . RIGHT NOW. https://www.empoweringparents.com

Love and Logic is a program and a book that will help you determine what type of parenting style you use, what will and will not work with your kids, and great comebacks every parent should know. https://www.loveandlogic.com

Heartlight Ministries

Mark and Jan Gregston are the founders of this amazing Christian program for kids in trouble. Heartlight also offers tremendous support for parents going through the worst nightmare of their lives. My son, Daniel, spent most of one year at Heartlight, located in Longview, Texas.

The atmosphere is beautiful with rolling hills, tennis courts, horses, and more. Mark and Jan's leadership skills, extensive understanding of troubled youth, and great unconditional love for teens is beyond outstanding.

We thank God for the influence and direction this program provided for my son during his time at Heartlight. I see many evidences of how God built admirable character qualities into Daniel's life as a result of Mark Gregston's influence and wisdom.

Why Choose Heartlight?

Heartlight's commitment to excellence is seen in the passion of our staff, the beauty of our facility, the success of our program and the effectiveness of our work with parents.

Heartlight has an atmosphere of relationship that creates an arena for change for your child. We are dedicated to offering hope to families in need.

(Who Endorses Heartlight?)

Dr. Josh McDowell: "I wish to God there had been a place like Heartlight for me when I was a teenager. I really do. It would have saved a lot of heartache for me."

Dr. James McDonald of *Walk in the Word* is the Founding and Senior Pastor of Harvest Bible Chapel. Though we didn't know James McDonald at the time, our whole family, all three children and all eleven grands, now attend Spring Lake Harvest Bible Chapel

Dr. Gary Smalley, Smalley Relationship Center: Gary is a best-selling author of more than sixty books, a world-renowned marriage and relationship expert, and a sought-after speaker with more than forty years of experience.

For more information and Endorsements for Heartlight go to http://www.heartlightministries.org

Acknowledgments

Walking through this cloud of confusion required much wisdom and support. They say you are blessed if you find one friend in life who is a kindred spirit. If you have just one friend who walks beside you, believes in you, encourages you, and even rebukes you when needed, you are blessed. And if you find that friend is ever faithful and true, you are blessed indeed.

God gave me more than one kindred-spirit friend for such a time as this. Many friends were there for me, believed in and encouraged me. Yet four women walked very close beside me during those years. The amount of pain I experienced was too much for me to bear alone. I took turns seeking counsel from my four friends so I didn't burn out any of them. They all brought rare and precious gifts to my life: faithfulness, encouragement, love, laughter, belief, kindness, and godly wisdom. God gave me more than I could have ever imagined or hoped for in you, my dear kindred-spirit friends: Sally Nickerson, Judy Skaff, Tracey Jackman, and Cathy Casazza.

Oh, the comfort, the inexpressible comfort of feeling

safe with a person, having neither to weigh thoughts nor measure words, but pouring them all right out, just as they are, chaff and grain together; certain that a faithful hand will take and sift them, keep what is worth keeping, and then with the breath of kindness blow the rest away.

Dinah Maria Mulock Craik

About the Author

I am a grateful daughter of the King of Kings, and it is to him I owe everything. As a wife, mother, nana, and devoted friend, my life is full. I am also a freelance writer, a helpmeet, a creator in the kitchen, a picture-painting enthusiast, and an active church member. My heart's desire is to make a difference in this world.

Most of my life I have been in ministry as a pastor's wife. I loved being my husband's biggest fan (he is an avid student of God's Word and an amazing, authentic teacher and communicator), and I felt complete as I served the Lord in the areas he gifted me.

As a pastor's wife, I have worn many hats throughout the years: a teen leader (I love teens!), Sunday school teacher, and director of children's programs (uncovering raw talent). I have led Bible studies for women, set up a MOPS program, and created Sunny Seniors to minister to the elderly. I laid the foundation for a couples Bible study and spent many hours ministering as a counselor and friend.

Writing is my passion. There is much power in the pen. My desire is to move, motivate, teach, encourage, celebrate, create, and share life through carefully chosen words.

Valuable life lessons learned through the fire refine us and make us fit to be used for God's glory. We can gain much through the messes of life. God never wastes a hurt, and he is faithful to work all things together for our good.

Should you connect with this book, I would be honored if you left your thoughts on my Facebook page: **Susan Jill Ream** I always respond.

May God's comfort and grace walk you through all the days of your life.

Blessing from the ever faithful, always kind Savior,

Susan Jill Ream

Made in the USA
Columbia, SC
14 December 2018